A TREASURY OF FLUTE MUSIC

In Progressive Order for Beginning Flutists

Transcribed and Adapted by Louis Moyse

G. SCHIRMER, Inc.

DISTRIBUTED BY

HAL•LEONARD®
CORPORATION
7777 W. BLUEMOUND RD. P.O. BOX 13819 MILWAUKEE, WI 53213

ED. 3064

about LOUIS MOYSE

Louis Moyse, the well-known flutist and pedagogue, has played under many famous conductors including Toscanini and toured worldwide with the celebrated Moyse Trio for many years. His talents as editor, composer and avid researcher in the field of flute literature are well represented in the Schirmer catalog. He is presently professor of flute and chamber music at the University of Toronto, Canada.

Contents
in Progressive Order

		Flute	Piano
ROMANCE *from: Lira Concerto*	Joseph Haydn	1	1
ARIA *from: Don Juan*	Wolfgang Amadeus Mozart	2	2
THEME *from: Variations on the name Abegg*	Robert Schumann	2	3
MENUETTO *from: Piano Variations*	Ludwig van Beethoven	3	4
MENUET *from: French Suite*	Johann Sebastian Bach	3	5
ALLEGRO NON TROPPO *from: Songs Without Words*	Felix Mendelssohn	4	6
BERCEUSE *from: Dolly*	Gabriel Fauré	5	8
LA GEMISSANTE (The Moaner)	Jean Francois Dandrieu	6	9
WALTZ	Franz Schubert	7	10
GAVOTTE *from: English Suite*	Johann Sebastian Bach	8	11
ANDANTE	Joseph Haydn	9	12
CONSOLATION (Theme)	Franz Liszt	9	13
POLONAISE	Carl Czerny	10	14
ALLEGRETTO *from: Fantasie Sonata No. 78*	Franz Schubert	10	15
ARIA *from: Oberon*	Carl Maria von Weber	11	16
ANDANTE *from: Piano Sonata, 4 Hands (K.381)*	Wolfgang Amadeus Mozart	12	17
THE POOR ORPHAN *from: Album for the Young*	Robert Schumann	12	19
ARIA *from: Sonata for 2 Violins & Continuo*	George Frideric Handel	13	20
MORNING *from: Peer Gynt*	Edvard Grieg	14	21
PAPAGENO'S LITTLE BELLS (Aria) *from: The Magic Flute*	Wolfgang Amadeus Mozart	14	22
TWO ECOSSAISE	Franz Schubert	15	23
TRIO *from: Novellette No. 1*	Robert Schumann	16	24
ANDANTE *from: Songs Without Words*	Felix Mendelssohn	16	26
GAVOTTE *from: Sonata for 2 Violins & Continuo*	George Frideric Handel	17	27
CAPRICCIO	Joseph Haydn	18	28
THEME *from: Piano Variations*	Ludwig van Beethoven	18	29
PRELUDE	Frédéric Chopin	19	30
POLONAISE *from: French Suite*	Johann Sebastian Bach	19	31
ALLEGRO *from: Trio for Flute, Violin and Continuo*	Georg Philipp Telemann	20	32
ARIA *from: Piano Variations*	George Frideric Handel	20	33
ANDANTE *from: Piano Sonata in E (Longo 23)*	Domenico Scarlatti	21	34
ANDANTE *from: Piano Variations*	Felix Mendelssohn	22	36
BAGATELLE	Ludwig van Beethoven	22	37
SOLVEJG'S SONG *from: Peer Gynt*	Edvard Grieg	23	38
ANDANTE *from: Piano Quintet, Op. 34*	Johannes Brahms	24	40
LARGO *from: Piano Sonata, Op. 58*	Frédéric Chopin	25	42
LE ROSSIGNOL EN AMOUR (The Nightingale in Love)	François Couperin	25	43

A Treasury of Flute Music

Romance
from: Lira Concerto

Joseph Haydn (1732-1809)
Transcribed and Adapted
for Flute and Piano
by Louis Moyse

47455c

Aria

from: Don Juan

Wolfgang Amadeus Mozart (1756-1791)

Theme

from: Variations on the name Abegg

Robert Schumann (1810-1856)

Menuetto

from: Piano Variations

Ludwig van Beethoven (1770-1827)

Menuet

from: French Suite

Moderato

Johann Sebastian Bach (1685-1750)

47455

Allegretto Non Troppo

from: Songs Without Words

Allegretto non troppo

Felix Mendelssohn (1809-1847)

Berceuse

from: Dolly

Gabriel Fauré, Op. 56 (1845-1924)

Andantino moderato

La Gémissante

(The Moaner)

Moderato

Jean Francois Dandrieu (1682-1738)

Waltz

Franz Schubert (1797-1828)

47455

Gavotte

from: English Suite

J. S. Bach

Andante

Joseph Haydn

Consolation

(Theme)

Un poco allegretto

Franz Liszt (1811-1886)

Polonaise

Allegretto moderato

Carl Czerny (1791-1857)

Allegretto

from: Fantasie Sonata No. 78

Franz Schubert

47455

Aria

from: Oberon

Carl Maria von Weber (Demersseman) (1786-1826)

Andante

from: Piano Sonata, 4 Hands (K. 381)

Wolfgang Amadeus Mozart

The Poor Orphan

from: Album for the Young

Robert Schumann

Copyright ©1976 G. Schirmer, Inc. All Rights Reserved. International Copyright Secured.

Aria

from: Sonata for 2 Violins and Continuo

Allegretto

George Frideric Handel (1685-1759)